Table of Contents

Table of Contents
Dedication 3
Disclaimer 4
Book Description 5
Introduction 6
   Growing up Twins 16
   Family Joys 21
   A Gentle Heart 25
   A Family Changed 29
Chapter Two- A Heart for Others 32
   A Young Man in Santa Monica 39
Chapter Three-The Turning Point 43
   A Heavy Loss 46
   A New Beginning 50
   Building A Life 53
   Michael's Legacy of Selflessness 58
Chapter four- The Disappearance 60
   Surviving on the Streets 62
   The Last Call 65
Chapter Five- Searching for Michael 67
   False Hopes 70
   A Spiritual Sign 73
Chapter Six -What We Know 75
   Painful Confirmation 79
   Elusive Answers 82
Chapter Seven- Unanswered Questions 85
   Harassment Hidden Truths 90
   Lingering Doubts 93
Chapter Eight -a Sister's Burden 96
   A Family Fractured 99

Chapter Nine- Chasing Clues 102
   Aloha House Confirmation 105
   Longs Drugs Survey 107
   Following the Path 109
   A Community Effort 112
   A Tantalizing lead 114
   A Case Stalled 116
   Systemic Failure 123
In Loving Memory 130
      Author's Note 131

Dedication

For Michael—
My brother, my heart, my missing piece. This book is for you. For your light, laughter, kindness, and your love that never dimmed, even when life was at its hardest. I write this not because I have all the answers, but because the world should know who you were.
Your missed more than words can hold and loved more than time can measure. Always.

Disclaimer

Disclaimer: This book reflects the author's personal experiences and beliefs. Some details, including descriptions of images and investigation findings, are based on publicly available information and personal accounts, and are intended to honor Michael's memory, not to accuse individuals without evidence.

Book Description

Missing Silenced Betrayed: The Michael David Long Story

Missing, Silenced, Betrayed: The Michael David Long Story is more than just a true crime account, it's a deeply personal journey of love, grief, and the fight for justice.
On July 23, 2019, Michael made his last phone call. Starving and sleeping on the ground, he ended with the words he always said: "I love you. I love you guys." Days later, he vanished.
Through the eyes of his sister, this memoir traces Michael's disappearance, the search for answers, and the painful years of uncertainty. It sheds light on a kind and vulnerable man, failed by the systems meant to protect him, and the relentless pursuit of truth in a world that too often forgets the fallen.
For anyone who has waited for a call, sought justice, or carried the weight of loss, this is Michael's story.

Introduction

The last time I heard Michael's voice was July 23, 2019. He called, weary and hungry. "I'm starving," he said, "sleeping on the ground." He'd never mentioned sleeping on the ground before, and it struck me as odd.". His raw honesty broke my heart, yet he tried to sound strong. He just needed someone to listen, care, and know he was still out there. I told him I have no extra money to spare; I have bills to pay. He said, 'Okay, thank you,' and I could feel him smiling—like when you just know someone is smiling through the phone." "Michael had a heart that never wavered. Even when life gave him little, he gave love."
As always, he ended with: "I love you. I love you guys."
Then, silence. Worry grew into dread. What followed was a nightmare no family should endure, searching, questions, and the crushing truth: Michael was murdered. His case remains unsolved.

This book recounts Michael's story from his sister's perspective. It covers his life, his struggles, his untimely loss, and the ongoing search for justice. Though the full truth may remain elusive, Michael's significance is undeniable. This is his story, and I am sharing it.

Before the questions, before the silence, there was Michael. And this is where his story begins.

Chapter One- A Boy Named Michael

Santa Monica: A Brother's Spark

 I was eight when Michael entered my life, born June 6, 1971, at Saint John's Hospital in Santa Monica, California. Mom didn't know she was having twins—one hid behind the other in her X-ray. When the first boy arrived, she laughed, "Who else is in here having a baby?" The doctor grinned, "Ma'am, you're having twins." Michael arrived four minutes later, small and perfect.

Mom let me name them—a gift that made me feel like the proudest big sister. From that moment, I knew Michael was mine to protect, to cherish. I dressed him carefully, fastening tiny buttons as Mom tended to his brother, an unspoken promise sealed between us.

Santa Monica was our world—sunlit sidewalks, the hum of street musicians, and a modest home filled with laughter and love. We found joy in small moments: the scent of the ocean drifting through open windows, the cool tile floors on scorching summer days, the way the radio crackled with old tunes as we danced through kitchen chores.

Michael's mischievous spark lit up our days, a grin always tugging at the corner of his mouth. He had this way of turning the ordinary into adventure—racing me to the end of the block just to hear me laugh, pretending the living room rug was hot lava we had to jump across. His joy was effortless, contagious.

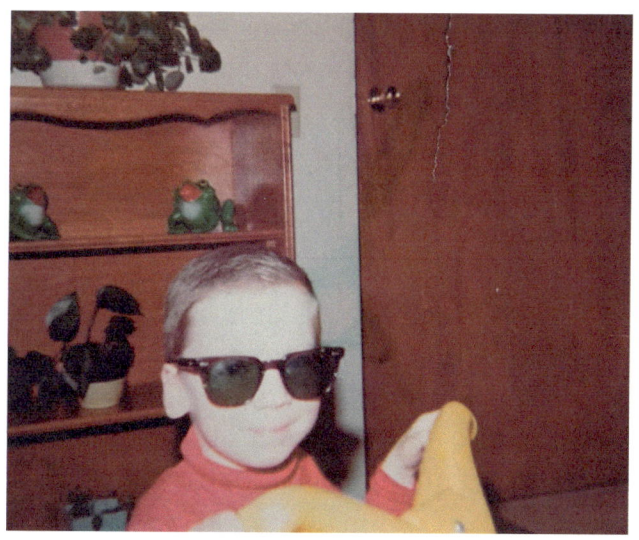

His love for potato chips, especially sour cream and onion—was almost legendary. He could eat them with the bagful.

I see him now, curled up on the couch, bare feet tucked beneath him, giggling at cartoons. The comforting scent of sour cream and onion drifts through the air, mixing with his laughter—soft, steady, familiar, like the gentle hum of home. We rode bikes through the neighborhood, pedals spinning wildly, the wind turning us into something weightless, free. Every sidewalk crack was a launch pad, every street corner an adventure waiting to unfold. When the sun dipped below the rooftops, we'd race home, breathless and exhilarated, the day's joy stitched into our skin.

Completing household chores took on an engaging character, resembling dance performances. The broomstick was effectively used as a microphone, the kitchen floor served as a stage, and the rhythm of sweeping blended with the melody from the radio. Observing this, our mother responded with a mixture of exasperation and amusement. "Michael performed with notable flair, reminiscent of a star on center stage, his laughter elevating the mundane to the extraordinary."

One summer day, when Michael was about 3, we took a trip to the Santa Monica Pier. He was obsessed with fishing, captivated by the mystery of what lay beneath the waves. Dad had bought him a little plastic fishing rod, red and yellow, too big for his small hands, but he held onto it like a treasure.

Standing at the edge of the pier, his grip tightened, his wide eyes filled with possibility. He didn't catch anything that day, but the world gave him something else—a symphony of ocean spray, the chatter of seagulls, and the thrill of waiting. His laughter echoed over the water, carried by the salt breeze, and even now, I can still hear it—the sound of pure, unfiltered wonder.

Another memory that stands out is our picnics. Mom would spread a blanket under a tree at Douglas Park or the beach in Santa Monica, and Michael would insist on helping her set up. He'd carry the smallest bowl of fruit, his face scrunched with concentration, determined not to spill a single grape. We'd spend hours out there, playing tag or pretending we were pirates on a ship, or rolling down the grass hills with

Michael always leading the charge as the fearless captain.

Michael Santa Monica ca 1973

His imagination was boundless, and his joy was infectious. Beach days were so much fun, we would go to the Santa Monica pier and ride the merry-go-round and get an ice cream cone or play games, the kind where you toss a dime in the dish and win that item or a ping pong ball in a goldfish bowl. I think we had more goldfish than anything, Mom used to say What are you going to do with the goldfish. Our mom was always happy to get some extra dishes.

Growing up Twins

Michael's fraternal twin brother was his shadow and rival. Their bond was complex—best friends one moment, bickering the next over who would carry the pizza in the house or Christmas toys, even identical ones. Typical sibling spats hid a quiet loyalty, shaping Michael's gentle heart. They were often mistaken for each other, a comparison that chafed, pushing Michael to carve his path.

On shopping trips, they'd scatter, hide in clothing racks, giggling as Mom and I chased them, or Michael would take off running one way and his brother the other way, half-laughing, half-exasperated.

  I remember one trip to the Third Street Promenade when they were about seven. The moment we stepped onto the bustling sidewalk, their eyes lit up, scanning the shops with a quiet excitement only mischievous kids could understand. They darted into a toy store, giggles trailing behind them, each disappearing behind a different display. Mom and I split up to find them, weaving through shelves stacked with stuffed animals and board games. Then—a muffled giggle. I followed the sound, stepping carefully past rows of colorful boxes until I spotted him—Michael, crouched behind a tower of board games, his hands clamped over his mouth to keep the laughter in.

When I pulled him out, his eyes sparkled with mischief, his face flushed with excitement. He leaned in, whispering like it was the most important secret in the world: "Don't tell him I'm here!" Those games of hide-and-seek weren't just fun, they were a constant, a way for them to test boundaries while staying close, knowing the other was always just around the corner.

That same sense of adventure followed them to school, where they perfected the art of swapping classrooms, fooling teachers with their identical grins.

Michael loved the game, thrilled by the rush of momentary deception, but he was never good at keeping secrets for long. His third-grade teacher, Mrs. Larson, once told Mom she'd never had twins pull off such a stunt so convincingly—until Michael, unable to resist, let it slip with a sheepish grin.

The freckle on his face always gave him away in the end. Even in mischief, Michael's honesty shone through—he loved the thrill, but he valued truth even more. It was a glimpse of the man he'd become—someone who believed in doing right, even when it cost him.

"At his birthday party, Michael got some cash and instantly turned into a comedy act—holding up a dollar bill to each ear and announcing, 'Look! I'm listening to my money talk!' Everyone burst out laughing, and honestly, he did look like the world's cutest little banker."

They took his life, but they can't erase his light. I carry it forward."

He didn't get the ending he deserved. But he had a beginning full of dreams, and a heart that never stopped hoping. That's the brother I miss—the one who believed in the road ahead

Family Joys

Dad's job at Northrop funded weekend adventures. A horse racing fan, he'd take me to watch the twins at amusement parks, their small hands gripping mine through crowds or on roller coasters.

Hollywood Park racetrack

Those days, sticky with cotton candy, glowed with joy, their sweetness lingering on our fingertips long after the last bite. Knott's Berry Farm was a world of wonder, where laughter tangled with the sounds of roller coasters and the scent of warm funnel cakes drifted through the air.
I remember the day Michael finally reached the height requirement for Ghost Rider, his excitement barely contained as we stepped into line. His fingers curled around mine, his small hand warm with anticipation. As the coaster climbed that first steep hill, he squeezed tighter, his breath hitching—but the moment we plunged, his scream turned into pure delight.

Wind rushed past, his laughter louder than the clatter of the tracks, his joy so infectious that I couldn't help but laugh with him.
The second we pulled into the station, he twisted toward me, eyes wide. "Again! Can we go again?" His exhilaration was endless, and so, of course, we went again.
Christmases were magic—late nights spent wrapping gifts, the soft glow of twinkling lights casting shadows on ribbon and bows.

Mom and I carefully folded paper over presents meant for two, each box mirroring the other.

But it was Michael's reaction that made every moment worth it.

One year, when he was five, we got him a toy racecar set he'd been eyeing for months. The second his hands tore through the wrapping paper, his whole face lit up, pure joy spilling over. Without hesitation, he dropped to the floor, setting up each track piece with intense concentration.

For hours, he raced those tiny cars, his voice mimicking the announcers he'd heard on TV—every turn, every near collision, narrated with the enthusiasm of a professional sportscaster. Mom and I sat back, sipping hot cocoa, watching him as the glow of the holiday lights reflected in his bright, eager eyes.

 Those moments—so simple, yet so vivid—are what I hold onto now. The sound of his laughter, the way joy came so easily to him, the way he made everything feel special. Michael and His Brother Christmas 1980's

A Gentle Heart

Michael's kindness showed early. He loved the gentle rhythm of fishing off piers, the soft pull of the tide beneath him, the way the world quieted when he cast his line into the water.

The lull of the waves was his refuge, a place where time slowed and the only sound was the occasional splash of something unseen beneath the surface. Later, that same love for stillness contrasted with his passion for NASCAR's deafening roar, the adrenaline-fueled energy of concert crowds—as if he thrived in both quiet reflection and unrestrained excitement.
No matter where life took him, he'd help anyone, no matter how small the need. At six, he disappeared from our babysitter's care, sending everyone into a panic. His brother searched frantically, the babysitter's voice sharp with worry, while Mom raced home, breath shallow, her mind spinning with worst-case fears. And then, there he was—sitting quietly on our apartment stairs, legs tucked under him, hands resting in his lap, staring off toward the street.

"I didn't want to be at the babysitter's," he said softly, his voice gentle, steady, unaffected by the chaos around him. He had needed solitude, a moment for himself, something the world didn't always understand but something he never stopped needing.
That was Michael—quietly retreating, always himself.
His empathy only grew with time, woven into every choice he made, every quiet gesture that showed how much he cared.

Michael is doing his homework at age 7

26

When he was eight, a neighbor's cat went missing, a small, nervous tabby that had darted out the door, vanishing before anyone could catch it. While others assumed it would find its way home, Michael refused to leave it to fate. He spent an entire Saturday combing the neighborhood, peering under porches, calling out in the softest voice, patient, unwavering.

Eventually, he spotted a pair of wide, wary eyes blinking up at him from the shadows. He crouched down, offering crumbs from his lunch, inching closer, whispering in a way that made the frightened animal trust him.

It took time, but Michael never rushed—he understood that some things, some moments, needed gentle patience Mrs. Carter, the cat's grateful owner, baked him a fresh batch of cookies—a warm, golden thank-you straight from the oven. But Michael, true to himself, didn't keep them for long. Instead of hoarding his reward, he passed them around, offering bites to friends, strangers, anyone who wanted one.

That was his always giving, always thinking of others, never expecting anything in return.

A Family Changed

In November 2000, Dad died at 71, worn out by heavy drinking. Six months later, in May 2001, Mom passed at 66, her stroke shrouded in questions. Medics asked Michael and his brother, "" They replied, "Nothing, she's having a stroke."

Michael Mom and I Christmas 2000 about 5 Months before she passed

Mom and Michael Christmas 2000 at my in-law's home

Michael and his brother shared a cramped one-bedroom apartment, each carving out their own space within its worn walls—his brother in the bedroom, Michael on the sofa, a quiet arrangement that spoke more to circumstance than comfort. The sofa was too small, its cushions worn thin, but Michael never complained. It was home, at least for now.

Both worked as movers, laboring under the relentless sun, their days defined by aching muscles, sweat-soaked shirts, and the rhythmic grind of truck engines waiting to be loaded. The job was demanding—each morning, they hefted dressers, couches, boxes filled with another family's memories, destined for new homes. But their own lives remained frozen in uncertainty, caught in a cycle that never seemed to lead anywhere new. Yet the real weight was never just in the boxes they hauled—it was in the unseen burdens Michael carried, stacked upon him like an ever-growing pile of loss. Grief settled deep in his bones, in the spaces between words unspoken, in the silence of long evenings spent staring at the ceiling. His relationship with his brother had always been a delicate balance—shared childhood mischief turned into strained adulthood responsibilities, their bond tested by exhaustion, by wounds neither of them knew how to mend.

Michael never complained. But the exhaustion showed in quiet ways sigh too deep for someone so young, the slow drop of his shoulders after another grueling shift. He had always been someone who carried too much, too much kindness, too much hope, too much of other people's struggles. The world never made room for that kind of heart.
And in the end, the world did what it always seemed to do, it took more than it gave.

Chapter Two- A Heart for Others

Finding Joy

Michael had always loved the idea of the open road, the promise of endless highways, new landscapes unfolding mile by mile. He dreamed of becoming a truck driver, getting his commercial license, and traveling across the country, seeing places he had only imagined through TV screens and passing conversations.

It wasn't just about the job, it was about the escape, the adventure, the ability to keep moving. He talked about driving through the wide stretches of Texas, watching the sun rise over Arizona's desert roads, stopping at small-town diners where no one knew his name but greeted him like family anyway.

Michael had always been someone who thrived in motion. Whether it was lifting furniture as a mover, losing himself in the energy of a rock concert, or feeling the rumble of racecars at the Speedway, he was happiest when the world was alive around him.

Though life pulled him in other directions, that dream stayed with him. Whenever he saw a semi-truck roll down the highway, he'd watch it with quiet admiration, imagining himself behind the wheel, hands steady, destination unknown but full of possibility.

Michael found joy in his passions. NASCAR races lit up his eyes, and whenever Jeff Gordon won, he'd call, voice buzzing with excitement, eager to relive every turn.

Michael at Nasar

Michael at the Auto Club Speedway in 2006, beaming with pure exhilaration, lost in the deafening roar of engines and the pulsing energy of the crowd.

That day at the Speedway wasn't just another event, it was a dream realized, the culmination of years spent watching races on TV with Dad, memorizing every turn, every strategy, every heart-pounding acceleration. He had always imagined what it would feel like to witness it in person—the rumble of the cars shaking through his chest, the scent of burnt rubber mingling with the warm California air.

When we finally went, that childlike awe returned in full force. Michael cheered louder than anyone, voices rising above the crowd, hands gripping the armrests as if holding onto the moment itself. The race unfolded in a blur of speed and thunder, and for once, life felt simple, light, unburdened.

During a pit stop, he turned to me, face lit up in a way that erased every hardship he had ever endured. "This is the best day ever," he said, and I knew he meant it. The engines screamed, the sun blazed down on the track, and in that instant, nothing else in the world mattered. I can still hear it—the deafening energy, the pulse of the track, the unfiltered joy of a man who had carried too many burdens, finally weightless for just a day.

Music pulled him into its embrace the same way racing did. Rock concerts were his sanctuary, the place where he could lose himself in sound, in movement, in the shared electricity of a packed crowd. I remember him saving up for months just to see Matchbox Twenty in 2003 at The Forum in Los Angeles—a ticket he guarded like treasure, anticipation carrying him through long shifts and hard days.

He came back buzzing with excitement, his voice hoarse from singing every lyric at the top of his lungs. "The bass shook the whole arena," he told me, eyes bright, arms moving as if replaying the way, the drums vibrated through his chest. In those moments, whether it was racing, concerts, or even football, Michael wasn't just watching, he was feeling, living, absorbing every ounce of joy the world had to offer.

Football fueled his cheers, a steady force that gave him space to exist beyond life's struggles. He never missed a Rams game if he could help it, shouting at the screen, his voice rising with every play, every near-miss, every heart-stopping comeback. Sunday afternoons weren't just about the sport—they were about the rush, the certainty that for a few hours, nothing else mattered. When the Rams won, Michael would throw his arms up, grinning like a kid, as if victory belonged to him too.
But his passions weren't confined to stadiums and roaring crowds. He loved history, the stories woven into ancient relics, the whispers of the past etched into artifacts.
I remember the day we went to the King Tut exhibit in Los Angeles. He moved

slowly through each display, his eyes scanning every detail, his hands resting on the glass as if hoping to absorb the history held within. He lingered at the golden mask, staring with quiet reverence. "Imagine being remembered for thousands of years," he murmured, his voice thick with wonder.

He saw history not as facts, but as people who had walked, laughed, fought, just as he had.

That was Michael—finding awe in everything, always ready to be amazed, no matter where life had taken him. Even in moments when the world weighed heavy, he carried that curiosity, that hunger to understand, to see the beauty in what came before him, and what was still to come.

He gave what he had, even when it wasn't much. A ride. A meal. A moment of peace. That was Michael—always reaching out, even when he was hurting too.

A Young Man in Santa Monica

Before his move to Maui, Michael spent his young adulthood in Santa Monica, balancing responsibility with dreams, carrying the same kind of heart that had always defined him.

His jobs were modest—delivering newspapers at dawn when the city was still wrapped in the hush of morning, bagging groceries in the afternoon beneath fluorescent lights, and even a brief stint as a lifeguard, scanning the waves from his station on the beach, always watching, always grounded by the rhythm of the ocean.

But his real love, his true sanctuary, was the sea. On his days off, he'd retreat to the pier, fishing rod in hand, watching the water shift and shimmer, endlessly restless, endlessly familiar.
Time slowed when he cast his line, the tension in his shoulders easing as he lost himself in the quiet patience of the tide.

When he could, he'd board all-day fishing boats, letting time slip away with the

current. The ocean soothed him, offering him the steadiness of life too often refused. He found comfort in its vastness, in its simple certainty—its endless rise and fall, its promise that no matter how rough the waves, the shore would always be waiting.
Yet, life wasn't always gentle. The loss of our parents hit him like a wave that never receded, pulling at his footing, leaving him struggling to stay upright.

He worked, he laughed, he found moments of joy, but I could see the quiet weight he carried, the strain beneath his easy smile, the way his eyes lingered in places they had once stood.
I remember one summer, when he was 22, he picked up painting—not because he thought he was an artist, but because he wanted to capture something beautiful in a world that often felt uncertain.
He'd sit on the beach with a cheap set of watercolors, dipping his brush into the tiny plastic tray, eyes squinting at the fading sun as if trying to memorize its colors before they slipped beneath the horizon. Every so often, he'd glance down at his paper, smirking at his own effort. "I'm no Picasso," he'd say, chuckling, "but it's fun!"

One day, he handed me one of his pieces—a lopsided depiction of the pier, the sun bright orange, sprawling unevenly across the sky.

Imperfect, yet so completely him. I still have it, tucked away in a box, a quiet treasure, a piece of him I never let go of. He created many other pieces, each one carrying something unspoken desire to create, to hold onto beauty even in the hardest times.
Michael also had a knack for making friends. He had this way of making people feel seen, whether they were tourists wandering the Promenade or the street performers strumming guitars near the boardwalk.
One of his closest friends, Tommy, who sold hot dogs near the beach, once told me Michael was the only person who ever asked how his day was going. That was Michael—always seeing people, always caring.
But beneath his warmth, I saw the weight of his struggles growing, especially after our parents were gone. He wanted so much to build something stable, something lasting—but life always seemed to throw roadblocks in his path. Still, he kept going, kept searching, kept hoping. Because that's who he was—a fighter, a

dreamer, and a man who never stopped finding beauty, even in the mess.

Chapter Three-The Turning Point

When Michael was about 14, his world suddenly shifted into the span of a second motorcycle accident that left him with a broken leg in two places, a moment that would mark him for months to come.

The crash was violent, unexpected, the kind of accident that leaves behind not just wounds but memories that linger in sharp flashes. He was rushed to the hospital, the pain radiating up his body in relentless waves, his leg twisted in a way that even he, always tough, couldn't ignore.

Doctors worked quickly, setting the bones, securing his leg, and preparing him for a long recovery ahead. What was supposed to be an active teenage year turned into a month-long hospital stay, confined to sterile walls, the rhythmic beeping of machines becoming his new background noise.

When he was finally released, his freedom came with limits—he was wrapped in an almost full-body cast, his leg locked in place, refusing him even the simplest movements. Walking, bending, stretching things he had taken for granted now seemed impossibly distant.
But Michael, ever stubborn, ever determined, found ways to adjust. He cracked jokes with nurses, learned the rhythm of navigating with his new restrictions, refusing to let frustration consume him. When friends visited, he grinned instead of sulked, leaning into conversation as if it were a lifeline.

He hated the cast—the weight of it, the stiffness, the way it slowed him down. But in classic Michael fashion, he never let it define him. If anything, it was just another hurdle, another battle to push through.

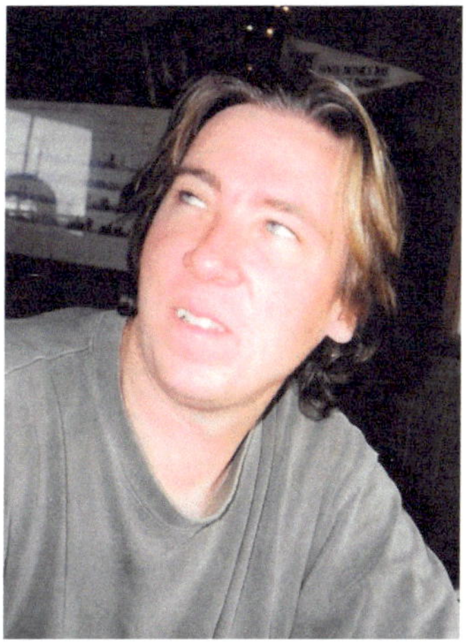

A Heavy Loss

After Mom's passing in 2001, something in Michael shifted—his world dimmed, and the light in his voice softened in a way I had never heard before. Losing both parents within six months was a cruel blow, unraveling the foundation he had always relied on, leaving behind a silence that stretched too wide to fill.
He worked hard, hauling furniture under the punishing heat, muscles aching, hands calloused from long shifts—but the heaviest weight wasn't the physical strain. It was the instability of a home that no longer felt like home, the shared apartment with his brother turning tense, fragile, heavy with unspoken grief.

Michael in 2003 working a moving job in Santa Monica

His voice—once mischievous, teasing, effortlessly alive—grew weary. "I'm just tired," he'd say, but it was more than exhaustion. It was a sadness sleep couldn't mend, a weariness that settled deep, in places even rest couldn't reach. Those years were hard to watch. Michael had always been the optimist in our family, the one who could find silver linings where no one else could. But after

47

Mom and Dad were gone, that light flickered, dimming slowly, unevenly, like a candle fighting against the wind.
He didn't call that often. Not about them, anyway.
When he did, it was about the car acting up, or the cat throwing up on his shoes again. Just enough to prove we were still tethered, but never long enough to slip into the deep end.
We didn't talk about Mom. Or Dad.
Not directly.
But sometimes I'd hear it in the way his voice caught before a joke, or how he paused before saying, *"So, how're you holding up?"*—like he wasn't just asking about the weather.
I'd answer lightly, careful not to crack the surface.
Because once you name the grief, it sits with you. And maybe we weren't ready to offer it a chair.
The distance—me out in Antelope Valley, him clinging to the ocean breeze in Santa Monica—wasn't just miles. It was everything we couldn't say. Micheal would always make appoint o stop by and see me when he did a moving job like on the way to Vegas.
By 2010, the moving business faltered, the last thread of stability slipping through his fingers. Michael lost the apartment Mom had left behind, and with it, another piece of his footing.

Adrift, searching for something steady, something safe, he kept pushing forward, even when the world seemed determined to push him down.

A New Beginning

Hoping for a fresh start, we saw Maui as a chance for Michael to rebuild. His relationship with his brother, now living in Maui, had frayed, but we thought the island's beauty and new surroundings might rekindle their bond and give Michael a better life. In 2010,

In 2006, a few years before his move to Maui, during a difficult time after our parents' passing.

I drove him to LAX for his flight, a knot in my stomach whispering I might never see him face-to-face again. Maui's allure felt like a promise of hope.

Michael arrived, and his brother picked him up. For a few weeks, things seemed okay. I spoke to them, urging patience as Michael adjusted. He told me about the island, the way the ocean sparkled, the smell of plumeria in the air. He sounded hopeful, and I clung to that.

But his brother grew frustrated, complaining that Michael wasn't job-hunting fast enough. Ignoring my pleas to give him time, he drove Michael to Kihei, dropped him off with just his cellphone, and left. Michael called, lost. "What do I do now?" he asked. My heart broke.

I sent money via the Western Union for food and promised to figure something out.

I spent hours on the phone with him, trying to map out a plan. I'd look up shelters, job listings, anything that might help. Michael was resilient, but I could hear the fear in his voice.

He didn't want to be a burden, but he didn't know where to turn. Those calls were agonizing. I wanted to fly to Maui and bring him home, but I couldn't afford it, and he wasn't ready to leave. All I could do was support him from afar, hoping he'd find his footing.

Building A Life

Locals near the beach welcomed Michael, sharing food and a spot by their tent. Mom always said life gave Michael the short end, and it stung me to see her words proven true. I posted Craigslist ads for yard work and moving jobs, ordered business cards, and coached him to seek referrals.

Michael landed a yard work gig, earning cash.

Days later, a retired lifeguard and his teacher wife, both in their mid-80s, offered him a room in their Hawaiian home for $500 a month, a steal for Maui. Michael was thrilled, and so was I. "See, I knew it'd work out," I told him.
For five years, Michael thrived. He poured himself into work, finding purpose in movement, in labor, in the satisfaction of a job well done. He bought gardening equipment piece by piece, each tool a quiet investment in the future he was building, his hands rough with effort but his spirit resilient.
He called me often, his voice bright with pride, every milestone proof that he was

making it, standing on his own, shaping a life that belonged to him.
The retired couple who took him in adored him, just as I did. They saw what I always knew—his kindness, his heart, his unwavering ability to give, even when life had taken so much.
I sent him care packages, small gestures to remind him he was loved, that I was thinking of him, that no matter how far we were, he wasn't alone. New gardening gloves so his hands wouldn't blister, a sturdy pair of boots so his steps were sure, a small radio so he could listen to music as he worked, the songs filling the quiet spaces of his days.

Every time, he'd call to thank me, his voice full of gratitude, almost surprised by the love poured into those boxes.
"You didn't have to do that," he'd say.
But I could hear it—the way it meant more to him than he let on, the way my small gifts wrapped around him like comfort, like home.

Here Michael bought a new phone and was so proud of his accomplishments he sent me a photo he was loving life in Maui Michael's kindness was not a fleeting gesture—it was the foundation of who he was. He understood struggle, the weight of uncertainty, and the sting of rejection. So, when his brother, now houseless, had nowhere else to go, Michael didn't hesitate. He offered shelter, a place where safety and dignity were not conditional. Later, when his brother introduced a woman in need, Michael once again opened his home, believing that compassion was meant to be shared.

But kindness is a fragile currency in a world that often repays it with betrayal. In 2016, everything shifted. The very people he had protected filed a restraining order against him. In a cruel twist, the space he had once offered so freely was no longer his.

The walls that had witnessed shared moments of hope now held him at a distance, as if he had become the intruder in his own life. The betrayal was swift and final, leaving him stunned in its wake. Desperate to make sense of it, he poured his pain into his medical records—a place where his voice, however broken, could not be ignored. The documentation did not simply list symptoms or statistics—it carried the weight of a man who had given everything and lost more than he could bear.

Each word was a testament to his devastation, a plea to be seen beyond the shadow of his circumstances.
With nowhere left to turn, Michael became houseless.
It was not just the loss of a physical space—it was the unraveling of his identity, the crushing realization that trust could be weaponized against him. The world had silenced him, dismissed

him, and now it watched as he struggled to exist.

Yet, even in the depths of this betrayal, he refused to disappear. He held onto fragments of himself, to the belief that his story was worth telling. And though the world had taken so much from him, it could not take away the truth.

This chapter was not just about his loss— it was the beginning of his fight to reclaim his voice.

Does this capture the depth you're looking for? I can refine it even more if you'd like! Let me know if there's anything specific, you'd like to emphasize.

Michael's Legacy of Selflessness

Michael's generosity had no limits. He wouldn't hesitate to give his last dollar, the shirt off his back, or even his only dry clothing if it meant sparing someone else's suffering. On the streets of Kihei, near the algae-choked ponds of Piikea Avenue, he saw a man—his friend—struggle, trapped in the slimy muck.

Without thinking, Michael jumped in, pulling him free with steady arms. He was drenched, the filth clinging to him, but that didn't matter.
What mattered was his friend, shivering and embarrassed. So, Michael did what only he would—he stripped off his own dry shorts and handed them over, an unspoken act of dignity and care.
That was Michael—fearless, compassionate, and selfless, even when he had little for himself.

His kindness echoed far beyond that moment. Others in Kihei spoke of the way he cared, even when no one asked him to. A woman at the market recalled the day he had shared his last sandwich with her, despite having gone hungry himself. A fellow houseless man spoke of the freezing nights, when Michael would place a blanket over him while he slept, ensuring that someone else had warmth before he did.

These gestures, the small, quiet ones, were the heart of who Michael was. He didn't seek recognition, nor did he ask for thanks. His kindness was instinctual, woven into the very fabric of his being.

And that is what I miss most. Not just his presence, but the way he made the world softer, kinder. His heart was his greatest gift, and though he is gone, his legacy of selflessness remains.

Does this resonate with the message you want to convey? Let me know if you'd like further refinements or additions! I'm here to make sure his story is told exactly how you envision it.

Chapter four- The Disappearance

The Distance Between Us

The restraining order in 2016 stripped Michael of his home, his stability, and the fragile security he had worked so hard to build. The streets of Kihei became his reality, a world with its own rhythm—one that demanded resilience. At first, he fought to keep going, but the weight of it all—the humiliation, the betrayal, the erosion of trust—began to wear him down.
Hard alcohol became his escape. It wasn't like before, when he'd sip on a cold beer after work, winding down from the day. This was different. It was a way to forget, to numb, to quiet the voices that reminded him of everything he had lost.

Mom's words echoed in my mind: *Michael always got the short end.* And now, I was watching it happen again.
I'd call whenever I could, hoping to reach him, to remind him that he wasn't forgotten. Some days, he'd pick up—his

voice heavy, weary, like the world had pressed against his chest too long. I'd ask him about his day, try to pull him into conversation, grasping for pieces of him that felt like they were slipping away.
And when he laughed—oh, that laugh. Even when life had stripped so much from him, that spark remained, if only for a moment. It reminded me of Michael, I had always known—the one who made people smile without even trying.

But the calls grew shorter. The spaces between them stretched wider. His words became distant, answers clipped, fading into something I didn't want to recognize—disconnection.
I kept calling. Kept trying. Kept holding onto the hope that he knew—*really* knew—that I was always here.
Because no matter how far he drifted, he was still Michael. And he was still my brother.
Does this resonate with the feelings and moments you want to capture? I can refine it further or adjust the tone to match your vision even more.

Surviving on the Streets

Michael found refuge at Saint Teresa's Church in Kihei, where he ate dinner and became a familiar face. The church was a small, white building with a red roof, nestled near the heart of Kihei, a place where the community gathered to support those in need.

Michael would sit at the long tables in the parish hall, sharing meals of rice, beans, and sometimes fresh fish donated by local fishermen. He told me once how the volunteers there made him feel seen, not as a houseless man, but as a person. "They know my name," he said, a small smile in his voice.
I sent care packages for his birthday and Christmas—shorts, t-shirts, gift cards, and once, a new baseball cap.
"Thank you," he said, chuckling, turning the cap over in his hands. "I'm not giving this one away."

Michael had a habit of passing things along sharing what little he had with others who needed it more. But this cap? This one was his.

For months after, I'd hear the slight smile in his voice when he'd mention it. "Still got the cap," he'd say, like it was more than just fabric—it was a piece of home, a reminder that someone cared.

Through everything—the long walks, the restless nights—he kept it. And somehow, that cap stayed clean and intact, like he protected it, held onto it as a small comfort against the world's harsh edges. I paid his cellphone bill for years to keep him connected. He'd call monthly, his voice a lifeline. "I'm okay," he'd say, even when I knew he wasn't.

When he went silent, I asked the Maui Police Department to check to see if he was okay since I had not heard from him. Once, they pinged his phone and found him, urging him to call. "It's hard to charge my phone," he explained, "and places are far to walk."

Those care packages were my way of holding onto him, of reminding him he was loved. I'd spend hours picking out the perfect items—bright blue shorts because he loved blue, a t-shirt with a palm tree. After all, it reminded him of Maui's beauty, a gift card to Longs Drugs so he could buy essentials.

Each package was a prayer, a hope that he'd feel my love across the miles. But as the years went on, I could sense his struggle growing, and the packages felt like a small bandage on a gaping wound.

The Last Call

July 23, 2019, 11:03 a.m. Pacific time. I was sitting in my car, just about to step into a store when my phone rang. Michael's voice was quiet, heavy in a way I hadn't heard before.
"I'm starving," he said. *"Sleeping on the ground."*

The words settled in my chest like lead. I wanted to fix it, to pull him out of the suffering he had been forced into, but I was drowning in bills myself. My hands gripped the steering wheel, wishing, begging for a way to change something.
"I'm sorry," I said, my voice barely above a whisper.]

He paused. I held my breath, waiting for the weight of his disappointment, his frustration, something that would reflect the unfairness of it all. But instead, he did what he always did.
He smiled through the phone.

"Okay," he said softly, like he was reassuring *me* instead of the other way around. *"I'll talk later. I love you. I love you guys."*
That was the last time I heard his voice.

Seven days later, on July 30, he signed up for the Ka La Hiki Ola mobile hygiene program in Kihei. They never saw him again.

I reply to that call in my mind every day. His exhaustion, the way he tried to ease my guilt, the quiet acceptance in his voice. I still wonder—if I had said more, done more, found some impossible way to get him off the streets *that day*, would things have been different?

That moment is a weight I carry, a shadow that lingers. But so are his words. *"I love you. I love you guys."*

A final gift, one last echo of who he was—his boundless love, his unwavering kindness.

And that, at least, is something I will never lose.

Chapter Five- Searching for Michael

Michael's silence in August 2019 unnerved me. He'd always call, even borrowing phones just to say, *"I'm okay."* That reassurance had become a rhythm, a lifeline. But suddenly, the calls stopped. His brother, incarcerated at MCCC for probation violations since April, continued calling—but his words unsettled me.

In May, he asked me to contact someone at Michael's former home about clothes. *Something about it felt wrong.* I tried anyway, but the number didn't work.

In June, his voice edged his voice.

He snapped, demanding that I stop Michael from saying he'd get *"life,"* then abruptly hung up. I turned the phrase over in my mind, unsettled. *Life?* What did he mean? Was it just an empty statement, or was there something deeper lurking beneath it?

In July, he called again, this time saying someone had stolen Michael's backpack.

The details were vague, the conversation abrupt. Each cryptic message chipped away at my sense of stability, layering fear on top of fear.
I spent sleepless nights piecing together his words, tracing their meaning like puzzle pieces that refused to fit. I called the number again, desperate for a connection, for answers. *Disconnected.*
I reached out to mutual friends. Had anyone heard from Michael? The response was always the same: Nothing. Each dead end felt like a punch to the gut, tightening the grip of fear I couldn't shake—was I running out of time?

On August 10, his brother, still at MCCC, sounded different. Hopeful.
"Michael entered Aloha House," he said, thrilled. "Rehab for alcohol issues."
Relief flooded in—I held onto that hope; let it settle like a fragile reassurance. But weeks passed. No calls, no messages, nothing from Michael. The silence felt suffocating.
I emailed Aloha House in September. No response. I called, left voicemails, waited. More silence.
Then, in October, his brother's voice cracked over the phone. "Something's wrong."
I wanted to file a missing person's report, wanted to throw caution aside and act.

But he urged me to wait. Michael is fine, he insisted.
I hesitated. Trusted his judgment.
But the dread never left me.
I kept calling. Kept waiting. Kept searching for a sign that Michael was still out there.
And with every unanswered call, that lingering fear settled deeper in my bones—what if this time, he really was gone?

False Hopes

By November 2019, his absence had become unbearable. Michael had always found ways to check in, even borrowing phones just to say, *"I'm okay."* But now, there was nothing—no calls, no messages, just a silence that grew heavier with every passing day.

A friend who served Thanksgiving meals at Saint Teresa's Church didn't see him that year. It wasn't just unusual, it was alarming.
Panic set in. I began calling every church, every shelter, every number Michael had ever used, grasping for any trace that he was still out there.
A man named Steve, a regular at the church meals, remembered him. *"He was a good guy,"* he said, sadness flickering in his eyes. The spoke of a meal they had shared once, a fleeting moment, but beyond that, he hadn't seen Michael in months. It was a small comfort. But it wasn't enough.

December came, and desperation pushed me further. I texted the last number Michael had called from. The owner denied knowing him but mentioned rumors about Aloha House. Rumors. That was all I had now.

I followed up, calling Aloha House again, clinging to the hope that someone would finally give me answers. This time, I reached a receptionist—but privacy laws stood in my way.

"I can't confirm or deny anything," she said flatly.

I pleaded with her, begged her to tell me anything—had Michael been there? Had he sought help? Had someone seen him? She wouldn't budge.

The walls kept closing in.

June 2020 brought another thread of hope—an outreach worker from the Family Life Center in Kahului called, believing she had found Michael.

"He's planning a trip to Colorado," she said.

Relief surged through me. Finally. Finally, something solid.

But then—Colorado? I corrected her. I'm in California.

A pause. Then reality shattered that fragile hope.

"I'm sorry. That was a 78-year-old Mike. Not yours."

The ground beneath me felt unsteady.

She mentioned one final detail—Michael had used their hygiene showers in July 2019. That was the last trace of him. After that, nothing.

Then, a woman from Michael's circle offered to call shelters on my behalf, a flicker of reassurance. But later, her words chilled me.
"He's deceased," she said, certainly in her voice.
She cited his four-year connection to Kihei, as if it were proof. But how could she know?
The weight of that declaration sat heavy in my chest.
Had I waited too long? Had the truth already slipped beyond my grasp?
I wasn't ready to accept it.
Not yet.

A Spiritual Sign

January 1, 2020. The first day of a new year, a time for fresh starts—but my heart still carried the weight of unanswered questions, of a search that felt endless, of a loss I wasn't yet ready to name.

I sat watching a psychic's live stream on Facebook, my mind distracted, heavy with thoughts of Michael. Then, out of nowhere, I froze.

"Do you know someone named Mike?" the psychic asked a woman.

She hesitated. No.

But the psychic only smiled.

"Mike is sending much love," he said.

The words sent a chill down my spine. She didn't know him. But I did.

It was as if, across an unseeable distance, Michael had reached through time, through space, through whatever lay beyond, to tell me what I already feared in my heart was gone.

I replayed the video over and over, listening for more clues, hoping for some hidden meaning in the tone, in the delivery. But there was only that single mention of his name, fleeting yet powerful, a whisper from somewhere beyond my grasp.

Was it coincidence? Maybe. But I couldn't shake the feeling that it was a message.
A final acknowledgment.
A sign that he was still with me, even if I could no longer reach him.
And in that moment, as grief settled into me, as reality began to take shape, I held onto those words.
"Mike is sending much love."

That was Michael—love, always love, even in the end.
And maybe, just maybe, it was his way of telling me to keep going. To keep searching. To keep fighting for the truth

Chapter Six - What We Know

A Haunting Discovery

February 13, 2020. The day I finally made the call.
Michael had been missing for months—long enough for fear to take root, for unanswered questions to become suffocating. His silence was unnatural, unbearable. I had exhausted every possible way to reach him, but now, the only step left was the one I had been dreading.
I called the Maui Police Department.
"I need to file a missing person's report." The officer on the other end questioned my grounds, his tone indifferent, weary—like he had heard this before.
"My brother is missing," I repeated, voice firm despite the lump tightening in my throat. *"I haven't spoken to him since July 23, 2019."*
A sigh. A pause. Then—recognition.
"The Long brothers," he muttered, recalling an incident. A fight, bruises. Michael refused to press charges.

It struck me, he remembered Michael, but not as I did. To him, my brother was a

case file, a fleeting recollection of past trouble. Not a person. Not a brother deeply loved, deeply missed.
I pressed forward, searching for leads.

Maui Memorial Hospital. Nothing. Aloha House. No answers. Privacy laws. Another roadblock.
February 19, 2020. Case #MP68153 officially entered the system.
It was real now. Official. But no closer to answers.
Then, in the dark corners of desperation, my husband opened a browser and typed the unthinkable:
"Unidentified bodies on Maui."
Because when the world refuses answers, sometimes the only choice left is to search for the worst possible truth.

Unidentified Dead Body Found in Maui   Unid Mex

This is what we found we have the Image hidden once
 I started sharing this info, they removed the tagline
A photo stopped us cold.
A body, face battered, jaw possibly broken, tattoos seemingly burned off.
I stared at it, heart pounding, breath caught in my throat.
My mind raced between logic and disbelief, flipping through every memory, comparing it with every photo I had of Michael, looking for proof that it wasn't desperate for any detail that would let me deny what I was seeing.
A law enforcement relative reviewed it, studying the same markers, the same wreckage.
"It's likely him," he said. And there is something weird going on in Maui
The words shattered something inside me.

The image haunted me. Guilt flooded in, drowning me in thoughts I couldn't escape.
As his older sister, I had always protected him. Kept an eye out. Fought for him.
So why couldn't I save him?

Sleepless nights followed, each one more suffocating than the last.
Scenarios played in my mind endlessly, twisting and turning.
What happened to him? Who hurt him? Was he scared?
I'd stare at that photo for hours, zooming in on every detail, searching for something to prove it wasn't him.
But deep down, I knew.
I had known all along.

Painful Confirmation

The call from the Maui Police Department came like a jolt—hope and dread crashing together in a way that made my stomach turn.

"I think we found Michael in custody," the officer said.
My heart raced. Had they really found him? Could it be that simple—that after months of searching, of restless nights and unanswered questions, I was finally about to hear his voice again?
But something inside me held hesitation.
"Does he have an eagle tattoo on his right arm?" I asked.
A pause. "No."
Relief flickered for a second—but only for a second.
"Are you sure?" I pressed. I described the tattoo in detail, the one that had been part of Michael since 1998. An eagle. Bold, detailed. A symbol of freedom—of everything he had longed for.

The officer reevaluated. His tone shifted. "Wait—it's his brother, not him."
Hope it shattered. Again.
I asked for photos, anything that could help me continue my search. The missing

persons posters I had sent to Maui shelters carried only fragments of his identity. A clear image of his tattoo would help.

The officer sent three pictures.

And there it was.

Michael's eagle tattoo. Bold, vivid, distinct.

I stared at the image, remembering the pride in his voice when he first showed me that tattoo all those years ago—how it had meant something to him, how he had carried that symbol like a piece of his soul. It was more than ink. It was him.

Then, my eyes drifted.

One photo, worn by hardship, lined by the weight of suffering, held marks and freckles that looked eerily familiar.

I zoomed in.

Then again.

My heart sank.

It matched. The freckles. The scars. The tattoo. Everything.

The body—the unidentified body—was Michael.

It was the proof I had been searching for, yet it was the proof I had never wanted to find

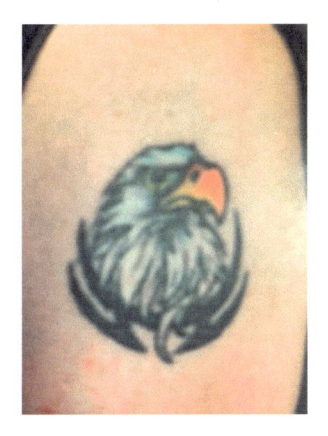

Michael's eagle tattoo on his right upper arm, inked in 1998, helped confirm his identity in my investigation.

They erased Michael's Life and made him disappear he was silenced and betrayed by people close to him and friends

Elusive Answers

March 2020. By then, Michael had been missing long enough for the weight of uncertainty to feel suffocating.
A wealthy friend whom he did work for in the past went looking, questioning three of Michael's associates near Longs Drugs in Kihei. Their response was frustratingly vague— "Claimed they saw him at Aloha House 30 days ago.
 Then he was MIA"

I doubted them immediately.
Something about their words felt rehearsed, as if they weren't telling me everything. And how could he have been at Aloha House 30 days prior, this was all when no one has seen Michael since last year in July?

I asked the friend to identify them from photos—if they truly knew Michael's whereabouts, I needed to know who they were. So, I could give the Information to the MPD, and I also asked if he would be willing to speak to the detective currently on Michael's case.

But he refused. *"I don't want to get involved in a police matter,"* he said, brushing off my urgency.
I pushed back, *explaining how critical this was*, how every second wasted meant less chance of finding Michael, but he wouldn't budge. His silence was its own kind of betrayal.
In May, I turned to Saint Teresa's Church, where Michael had often gone for meals. I spoke to the cook, hoping for clarity, for a sliver of information that might make sense of the tangled accounts I had been given.
"I haven't seen him in months, in a really long time " the cook said. Another dead end.
Then, in April 2020, Michael's brother, recently released from MCCC, heard from a security guard that Michael had been at Saint Teresa's 30 days earlier. That did not even make sense!

These conflicting timelines unraveled any hope of pinpointing his last whereabouts.

Where had he truly been?
Had anyone seen him, or was the truth
buried under rumors and half-memories?

I refused to stop searching.
I called the cook again, pressing for any
conversation, any name, any clue. He
hesitated, then finally said: He recalled
the last time he saw Michael a month and
months ago that
"He was quieter than usual. Sitting alone
at the edge of the table."
Such a small detail.
But it painted an image I couldn't shake—
Michael, withdrawn, distant, slipping
away even before anyone realized he was
truly gone.
I clung to every scrap of information,
hoping, wishing, that something would
finally lead me to the truth

Chapter Seven- Unanswered Questions

Seeking Beyond

By July 2020, desperation had pushed me into unconventional territory, the kind that most would dismiss, but I couldn't afford to.

I turned to remote viewing and psychics, chasing the possibility that someone—somehow—might see what I could not. The first remote viewer described a scene that chilled me to my core:
"Michael, struggling with self-doubt, was lured into a black van—once white, its VIN altered.
He was drugged, brought up to a very high cliff it was quiet, and she could feel the wind and he shot, in the back of the head and thrown from a cliff into the ocean." She said she was falling and falling then hit the water.

His wallet, she said, fell out of his pocket and got lodged among smooth gray rocks below jagged cliffs.
Two men, finding it humorous, were involved.

She provided two sketches of the men. (Note the sketches are posted on Michaels missing on Maui Michael David Long Facebook Page)

But what could I do with faces, with figures that resembled people who might not even exist? Accusing lookalikes without evidence felt reckless, and yet—the details were too specific to ignore.

Then, another psychic—unaware of the first—spoke.

"A black van. A brutal, ritualistic beating—humiliating, cruel, fueled by greed."

And then, one word. "Wharf."

Michael kept repeating it.

"Wharf."

And then, the details came—horrific, unbearable truths that shattered any lingering hope I had left.

They were betting on how long it would take him to die.

They were torturing him, dragging out his suffering as if it were a game.

And in those final moments, he prayed to God for mercy.

He begged.

And then—he passed quickly.

But even in death, the cruelty didn't stop. His body was so damaged, so broken, that when he reached the other side, he didn't want to be there.

He wanted to come back.

But he couldn't.
And the worst part?
They kept torturing him, unaware that he was already gone.
They didn't know.
They didn't care.
I didn't understand what it meant—not yet—but something about their shared visions, their mirrored details, stunned me.
Fueled me.
I reached out again, pressing for more details.
The first psychic, the remote viewer, described a specific cliff near yet she had no idea where in Maui it would be—jagged rocks, a sheer drop into the ocean, waves crashing violently below.
I turned to Google Earth, tracing her words like a map, scanning the coastline all around the island and desperate for anything that matched.
The psychic's voice was steady, but there was something in her tone—something unsettled, as if even she couldn't believe what she was seeing.
"One of them—he's massive. Built like a wrestler."
Then, almost to herself, she muttered: "What is this guy, a wrestler?"
The sheer size of him struck her. It wasn't just that he was big—it was that his presence carried an intimidating force,

something overpowering, something meant to instill fear.
Then, the second man.

"He's missing a tooth."
A small detail, but one that made him distinct. A marker. Something tangible that could have identified him—if only I had more to go on.
I sat with those descriptions, turning them over in my mind, searching for connections.
Had Michael ever mentioned men like this?
Had anyone in Kihei seen them before?
The psychic didn't hesitate—she was certain.
And that certainly made it even more chilling.
These weren't just vague figures in a vision.
They were real.
Somewhere, they existed.
And they had been part of Michael's final moments.
I searched.
I studied locations.
But nothing concrete surfaced, and yet—these visions gave me direction, a fragile thread to follow when all else seemed lost.
The Maui Police Department didn't care.

They don't use psychics, don't consider them credible.
To them, Michael was just a missing person.
And going missing isn't a crime.

Harassment Hidden Truths

I combed through every corner of the internet, convinced that Michael's disappearance wasn't just a tragedy, it was something far more sinister.
I posted missing persons flyers on Craigslist in Maui, hoping—praying—for leads.
Instead, the messages started.
Hundreds of emails. All from the same sender.
"You have no proof, and it won't hold up in court," one taunted.
Then came the worst of them.
"I beat his brains in and tossed him into the hole he crawled out of. He was dead when I left."
Another:
"He was thrown into the ocean."
And then—
"We pee on his grave every day."
Each email felt like a dagger. Each one laced with malice, designed to break me down.

What struck me most wasn't just the cruelty—it was the accuracy.

The details matched Michael's medical records of assaults. The body photo injuries aligned eerily with what was described.

One email suggested his body was buried at his former Eleu Avenue address—a place known to house men with criminal records.

I pushed for a search. A detective brought a cadaver dog.

The results? Negative.

But I couldn't shake the feeling, was the search thorough enough? Or had they overlooked something?

The threats kept coming. Emails are relentless.

Every morning, I woke up dreading what would be in my inbox.

One claimed to know exactly where Michael's body was.

I spent hours analyzing each message—comparing details, cross-referencing with what I already knew.

But deep down, I couldn't shake the terrifying thought:

Was I being taunted by someone who knew the truth?

Someone who wanted me to suffer?

Someone who knew me? I do feel it was two people that I know part family they said things that only a certain person would know.

I gave the information to the Maui Police department and told them who I thought it was, and they just brushed it off. They certainly could have questioned these two about but so much in my brother's case was never followed up on.

Lingering Doubts

Michael's medical records from 2016 to 2019 are filled with entries that read like warnings no one heeded. Assaults—some by unknown attackers. Unexplained injuries. Attacks unreported.
Each entry felt like a puzzle piece, a glimpse into something too dark to ignore.
Had someone been targeting him?

Had these assaults led to something worse?
I've shared his story everywhere—on the Missing on Maui - Michael David Long Facebook page, with police, with shelters videos
And still—no real action. No urgency. No answers.

The questions burn inside me:

- Why wasn't Michael's case prioritized?
- Who saw him last?
- Who sent those chilling emails? Deep down I know who did

Michael and his brother shared a childhood, their bickering typical, but this book seeks truth, not blame.
The body photo.
The tattoo confirmation.
The emails filled with grotesque details that match his medical records.
Someone knows more.
Fighting Against Silence
I've often wondered about the police's handling of Michael's case.
Why did it take so long to investigate?
Why weren't his associates near Longs Drugs questioned more thoroughly?
I have emailed the Maui PD countless times—each time speaking to a new officer, each time re-explaining everything from the beginning, and resending emails all I have found
It's exhausting.
One detective seemed genuinely invested, someone who cared, but after a few months—he was reassigned.
Then, silence again.
The lack of continuity. The lack of urgency.
It's infuriating.
I know Michael's case isn't the only one, but he deserved better.
He deserves Justice
Every missing person does.

Chapter Eight -a Sister's Burden

Carrying Weight

The tattoo photos and body confirmation shattered me. Seeing Michael, worn and broken at 48, fueled endless questions:

Who did this?
Where are his remains?
The harassing emails, cruel and knowing, deepened my fear that the truth was being buried—hidden beneath silence, beneath indifference.
As his older sister, I always felt responsible for his safety.
Guilt consumes me.
Could I have brought him to Los Angeles sooner?
Could I have saved him?
Sleepless nights replay the what ifs, but I channel them into resolve.
Michael's kindness, his fight to rise, fuels me.
I will keep searching—for him, and for every family who miss a name.
Because his story isn't over.
Not until justice comes.

The Weight of Guilt
It follows me every day.
I think about all the times I could have done more—
Called more often.
Sent more money.
Flown to Maui to bring him home.
I remember a conversation in 2018.
Michael, voice tired, spirit weary, said:
"I just want to rest." He wanted a place to lay his head
I promised I'd find a way to help him.
But I didn't act fast enough.
And now, he's gone.
That failure haunts me—but it also drives me.
I can't change the past, but I can fight for his future.
For justice.
For answers.

For his memory to be honored.
A Voice of the Missing
I've become an advocate for missing people, sharing Michael's story, and others like his.
Every time I speak his name, I feel him with me, urging me forward.
I've met other families—people who know this pain too well. They inspire me.
We share a bond no one should have to understand.
The pain of not knowing.

The endless search for closure.
But we also share something more.
Hope.
And that's what keeps me going.

A Family Fractured

Michael's disappearance didn't just break my heart—it fractured our family.
My relationship with his twin brother unraveled under the weight of unspoken questions.
I'd ask—What were Michael's last days like?
Did he say anything strange?
Did he seem scared?
Each time, his brother shut down.
But the silence hurt.
We would argue.
Me, pushing for answers.
Him, retreating into anger, denial.
We no longer speak.
How Loss Changes Everything
My own life shifted in ways I never expected.
At work, I struggled to focus—my mind, always drifting to Michael.
I never imagined I'd have to face something like this. You hear about tragedies in other families; think it's something that happens to someone else. But now—it's here. And it's the hardest thing I've ever had to endure.

On windy afternoons, I'd hear his laugh—
soft, familiarly to be reminded, over and
over, that he was gone.
My husband tried to support me, but I
knew it was hard for him—to watch me
unravel, to see grief pull me into a place
he couldn't reach. and he really got tired
of hearing me talk about it he just did not
want to deal with it.
The pain never fully leaves.
It's part of me now.
A scar that holds both the ache of loss and
the fight for justice.
Honoring Michael, Finding Purpose
But grief is not just sorrow.
It is love, preserved. A little brother gone
too soon
I became an advocate for missing people
sharing Michael's story and others like
his.
I launched a small blog, writing about
loss, about the agony of waiting, about
how the missing is not forgotten names,
but people—someone's child, someone's
brother.

Whenever I speak Michael's name, I feel
him near—not gone, just shifted into
memory, urging me forward.
I have met other families.
Missing on Maui.
Their strength astounds me.

We share a bond that no one should have
to understand—the pain of not knowing,
the endless search for closure.
But we also share hope.
And that is what keeps me going.

Chapter Nine- Chasing Clues

Medical Records and Heartbreak
I knew medical records could hold clues, but HIPAA made them nearly impossible to obtain.
I had to prove Michael was deceased—and that haunting photo of the unidentified body was enough.
December 17, 2020.
I received his records from 2016 to 2019—and they broke me.
Each entry painted a grim picture:
Michael was assaulted repeatedly.

- Sucker-punched.
- Pushed off a bus bench.
- His head struck.

- His foot crushed in 2019.

He visited Maui Memorial Hospital's ER often—each visit a record of his condition worsening.
Some reports noted he refused to name his attackers.
Why? Was it someone close to him?
Was he protecting someone? Or was he threatened into silence?
One detail stood out—he listed me as his contact, not his brother.
Even in pain, even as the world beat him down, he wanted me to know—even if he never truly said it.
But instead, he always told me, "I'm fine."
Even when he wasn't.
Even when he was broken, hurting, alone.
He hid his suffering to spare me.

The Worst of It

One record from 2018 shattered me.
Michael had been found unconscious near a park—his face swollen, ribs bruised.
The doctors noted he had been drinking heavily likely to numb the pain, both physical and emotional.
I sat with that report, staring at the words—trying to picture it, trying to imagine what he had endured in those final moments before collapsing.
Had anyone helped him? Had anyone seen?

Or had he simply lain there, bleeding,
alone, waiting for someone to find him?
I cried—not just for what had happened,
but for what I hadn't known.
Had I known, I would have dropped
everything.
I would have been there.
I would have held his hand and told him
he wasn't alone.

Aloha House Confirmation

Aloha House Confirmation
The medical records revealed what I had been chasing for months—a critical clue. August 14, 2019, 5:05 p.m.—Michael was in the ER, requesting transfer to Aloha House's Licensed Crisis Residential Services (LCRS).
It confirmed the rumors. He had been there.
But Aloha House had stonewalled me, hiding behind privacy laws, even when regulations required disclosure for missing people.
This time, I wasn't backing down.
I called.
"If you don't tell me the truth, I will see you in probate court. And then you will have to tell me."
Silence.
Then, movement.
They connected me to an outreach worker, someone named in Michael's records.
At first, he remembered "Mike Long, the pro golfer."
Not my brother.
I clarified.
He paused—then said:
"Michael stayed two days and left on August 16, 2019."

"He ditched them. Walked away. Happens all the time."
A common occurrence.
That phrase sat heavy in my chest.
Was that how they saw him? Just another name on a list, another person struggling to fight an impossible battle, walking away into uncertainty?
I pressed for more.
"Did Michael say where he was going? Did he seem scared?"
The worker thought for a moment.
"He was quiet. Almost resigned."
"Didn't talk much."
"But he kept saying he wanted to get better. For his family."
I held onto those words, letting them settle deep inside me.
Even at his lowest, even when everything was slipping, he was still thinking of us.
I thanked the man.
But I left the call with more questions than answers.

Longs Drugs Survey

Tracing His Last Steps
I accessed Michael's email, the one I had set up for him back in 2010 for Craigslist job ads.
I never expected it to lead me here.
Buried in the inbox were survey receipts from Longs Drugs, placing him at specific locations:
- 41 E Lipoa St, Kihei
    - March 18
    - March 21
    - April 18
    - June 27, 2019
- 275 W Kaahumanu Ave, Kahului
- June 9
- August 14 (8:59 p.m.)
- August 17 (8:59 p.m.), 2019

My hands trembled as I stared at the timestamps.
August 14, 2019.

Medical records showed he was discharged from the ER at 5:05 p.m. under a crisis worker's care.
Yet here was a survey receipt, placing him at Longs Drugs in Kahului at 8:59 p.m.
Had he left Aloha House already?
Was it truly him, or another Michael Long?
Then, August 17th receipt—the last trace of him.

107

After two days at LCRS, the system lost track of him, except for this one digital footprint.
And then, nothing.

The Unanswered Questions
I mapped out each location, trying to reconstruct his movements, looking for patterns, for meaning.
The Kihei Longs Drugs was near where he often stayed, a place he knew well, where he went for essentials.
But Kahului was different—farther, somewhere he only went when he needed something specific or was already in that area for services.
Was he passing through, heading somewhere?
I couldn't contact the stores to ask if anyone had seen him—it was too late, and surveillance footage, if it had ever existed, was long gone.
Still, those receipts were a lifeline.

A tangible connection to Michael's last days, scattered fragments of where he had been.
There weren't enough.
But they were something.

Following the Path

I never expected an old email account to become a gateway to Michael's final days. Back in 2010, I had set up his email for Craigslist job ads—just a simple tool to help him find work, nothing more.

Now, it was all I had left of him.
As I searched through his inbox, scanning for any digital footprint, I found survey receipts from Longs Drugs—timestamps placing Michael at specific locations in 2019.
A record.
I stared at the timestamps.
On March 18, he had been at Longs Drugs. Just another ordinary day.
Back then, I hadn't thought twice about where he might have been, what he was doing, whether it mattered.
But now, I see it differently.
Now, it was evidence—a timestamp marking a moment he had still been here.

The August 14 Puzzle
Then, one entry stopped me from cold August 14, 2019, at 8:59 p.m.
Medical records showed he had been discharged from the ER at 5:05 p.m. under crisis care.
Yet here he was—at Longs Drugs in Kahului, just hours later.
Had he already left Aloha House?

Had someone taken him there?
Or was it another Michael Long,
complicating the search even further?
I needed answers, but all I had was this
haunting inconsistency.
Then came the August 17 receipt—the last
digital trace of him.
After two days at LCRS, his movements
faded from the record.
No confirmed sightings.
No responses from the shelters.
Just this final timestamp before
everything went silent.

Mapping His Last Known Locations
I pulled up maps, tracing each Longs
Drugs, trying to reconstruct his
movements.
The Kihei location was near where he
often stayed, a familiar place where he
went for essentials, supplies, routine
survival.

But Kahului was different—farther,
somewhere he only traveled to when he
had a reason.
Had he been passing through? Headed
somewhere?
If I had discovered this sooner, I could
have called the stores, asked if anyone
had seen him, checked for security
footage.

But now it was too late.
The doors to answers had already shut.
Still—these receipts, these timestamps,
were something.
A lifeline, a record, proof of existence.
There weren't enough.
But that was all I had.

A Community Effort

A Community That Cared
As the weeks turned into months, local businesses stepped up in ways I never expected.
A coffee shop in Kihei kept Michael's missing persons flyer displayed in their window for months—long after most posters would have been taken down, long after most people might have moved on.
The owner, a kind woman, never stopped hoping.
Whenever she heard a rumor, she would call me, sharing whatever fragments of information she had.
Most leads went nowhere—false sightings, secondhand whispers, fleeting moments of hope followed by disappointment.
But that didn't matter.
What mattered was her effort—her belief that Michael still deserved to be looked for, to be remembered.
What mattered was knowing he had a community rooting for him, even if they couldn't bring him home.

Finding Strength in Others
Every time I spoke with her, every time I saw another flyer taped to a storefront, I

felt something shift inside me reassured me that I wasn't alone in this fight.

In a world where missing person's cases often fade into silence, these small gestures kept Michael's name alive.

The kindness of strangers, the shared humanity in a simple act of putting up a flyer, meant more than anyone could know.

Even when the leads didn't bring answers, they brought something else—connection, support, a reminder that Michael was not forgotten.

And that was everything.

A Tantalizing lead

Late 2024.
By now, time had stretched out, placing more distance between Michael's disappearance and the answers I so desperately sought.
I texted a woman close to Michael's brother, telling her I needed to know the truth—not just for closure, but because I couldn't leave this earth without answers.
Her reply was immediate.
"I cry daily over it."
Then, something I wasn't expecting.
She mentioned a man found drowned on May 5, 2020—someone who had hung around their group.
And before his death, he had said something chilling.
"Michael was badly beaten."
My heart pounded.
Someone had seen it. Someone had known.
This wasn't speculation. It was confirmation.
I pressed further.
"Do you know who did it?"
She hesitated.
"It was someone we both know."
But before she could say the name, she stopped.
"My phone needs charging."

And just like that, the conversation ended—another agonizing half-answer, dangling just out of reach.
She never followed up.
Never send the name.
Never gave me what I had been fighting for all these years.
The Silence That Shields the Truth
Her fear, her silence, it's what keeps Michael's case unsolved.
It breaks my heart—knowing that somewhere, people hold the pieces, but they refuse to place them together.
I still hope she'll find the courage to come forward.
That she'll say his name, say their names, and finally let the truth out into the light.
Until then, I kept searching.
Because Michael deserves answers.
And I won't stop until I have them.

A Case Stalled

May 22, 2025.
Michael's case is now on its fourth or fifth detective—I've lost count.
Each time, the process starts over.
I resend 27 emails containing every detail I've collected:

- Medical records documenting his assaults.
- Longs Drugs surveys placing him at specific locations.
- Harassing emails, filled with threats and cruel admissions.
- Psychic leads, though the police dismiss them entirely.

I lay out the facts, the evidence that should demand action, but nothing moves forward.
The Truth Is Clear, But the Case Remains Stalled
The photo of the battered body, matched by Michael's tattoo and freckles, confirms he was murdered.

Yet, officially, he's still listed as a missing person (Case #MP68153).

The Maui Police Department has followed a few leads—

- A drone scan over Piikea Avenue ponds, based on a tip.
- Cadaver dog searches of Eleu Avenue and Aloha House.

But nothing was found.
I question the thoroughness of these efforts.
Had they searched deep enough?
Had they dismissed possibilities too quickly?
Michael mattered.
Every missing person, every victim of a crime—deserves justice.

Fighting a Broken System
I have not met with every new detective on Maui, but I keep a binder of evidence—everything I've uncovered, everything I've pieced together.
It sits ready, waiting for someone willing to truly investigate.
But months pass without updates.
No phone calls.
No progress.
Just silence.
The lack of continuity, the constant turnover, the dismissal of key evidence, it's a system that feels broken, leaving families like mine trapped in limbo.
It's obvious that they don't care about Michael's case.

Not the way they should.

Justice, If Not in This Life, Then in the Next
As of today:
- No one has been arrested.
- His remains have not been found.
- The truth remains locked away.

I know in my heart Michael was beaten to death.
The photo confirms it.
The patterns of violence, the cruel messages, the things I've uncovered, they all lead to one conclusion.
I hope and pray that one day those responsible will be known that justice will find them.
If not here, then before a higher power—because Michael's story won't fade.
Not while I still breathe.

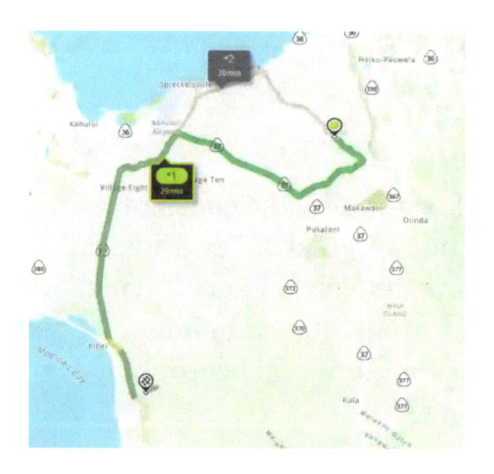

A map of Kihei, A map showing where Aloha house is and how far he would travel he more than likely went to Kahului, not Kihei, as shown

Chapter Ten- A Call to Action

The Broader Crisis

Michael's story is not unique, and that is the most painful truth of all.
According to the National Missing and Unidentified Persons System (NamUs), over 600,000 people go missing in the United States each year—a staggering number. While many cases are resolved, thousands remain unsolved, their families trapped in uncertainty, searching endlessly for answers that never come.

Among them are individuals like Michael—houseless, struggling with addiction, abandoned by systems meant to protect them.
For them, disappearance isn't just an event, it's a quiet erasure, a vanishing into the cracks of society, where few look and even fewer care.

True Crime vs. Reality
The true crime genre often transforms tragedies into entertainment—stories designed for suspense, for mystery, for the thrill of discovery.
But for families, it's not a plot—it's a nightmare.
A cycle of false hope, unanswered phone calls, dead-end leads, bureaucracy, dismissal.

And their case files just stacked on shelves in cold case unit with no answers and sometimes remain unsolved for many years

I've learned so much about this crisis through my search for Michael.
I've met mothers who've lost sons, siblings who've lost brothers—all of us bound by the same pain, all of us fighting to keep our loved ones from becoming statistics.

I heard a statistic that still haunts me: Less than 1% of missing people's cases involving houseless individuals are solved.

Why They're Forgotten
The reasons for this horrifying failure are complex:
- Lack of resources—Cases involving houseless individuals rarely receive the same attention as those from more privileged backgrounds.
- Societal stigma—These victims are often dismissed; their disappearances viewed as inevitable rather than urgent.
- Overwhelmed police departments—Detectives rotate, cases get lost, leads fade into

> stacks of paperwork until no one is
> left searching.

But the result is always the same people
as Michael is forgotten.
Unless we refuse to let them be.

Systemic Failure

Michael wasn't just failed by individuals—he was failed by the systems meant to protect him.
At every turn, resources fell short, leaving him without the support he desperately needed:

- Houselessness services in Maui were underfunded, meaning shelters were overwhelmed, beds were scarce, and outreach was limited.
- Addiction treatment programs like Aloha House had long waitlists—and even when he finally got in, he was released too soon, back onto the streets with nowhere to go.
- Law enforcement, stretched too thin, didn't prioritize his case—to them, he was just another statistic, rather than a man who deserved answers, justice, and dignity.

Michael wasn't invisible, but the system acted as if he was.

The Bias in Missing Persons Cases

Through my search for Michael, I've seen the failures firsthand.
Advocates across the country have confirmed this pattern—the way certain cases get attention while others are dismissed.

Michael—houseless, struggling—fall into the cracks of an indifferent system.
The reasons are many:
- Media bias—stories that fit a narrative of innocence and tragedy get airtime, while others are viewed as complicated, unworthy of headlines.
- Police resources and priority-houseless individuals, those battling addiction, are often treated as people who chose their circumstances rather than victims of larger failings.
- Public perception—certain victims garner sympathy, while others, unjustly, are ignored, judged, and forgotten.

But in every case, every missing person, every murder, every life lost—should matter the same.
This failure is not just about Michael—it's about the many who never get their justice.

Justice Shouldn't Be Selective! But it is!
I will not stop fighting for Michael, and I know there are families just like mine, trapped in the same cycle—searching, begging for answers, ignored at every turn.

We must fix this system—not just for those we've already lost, but for those who still need saving.

Because every person deserves to be found.

How to Help
If Michael's story has moved you, there are ways to make a difference—not just for him, but for the countless missing people whose cases remain unsolved.

Provide Information
If you know anything about Michael's case (Case #MP68153), please contact:
- Maui Police Department at 808-244-6400
- National Missing and Unidentified Persons System (NamUs) at https://www.namus.gov

Even the smallest detail could be the breakthrough needed to uncover the truth.

Support Missing Persons Initiatives
Beyond Michael, there are organizations tirelessly working to solve missing

persons cases and support families in need. Consider:
Volunteering with groups like [The Doe Network](#) or [The Charley Project](#), which focus on tracking and identifying missing persons.

- Donating to local shelters and addiction recovery programs—places that offer a lifeline to people at risk of disappearing into the system.

Advocate for Systemic Change

Justice for missing people requires more than just search efforts, it requires structural change:

- Push for increased funding for missing people's units to ensure cases like Michael's get the attention they deserve.
- Advocate for better police training on handling cases involving vulnerable populations, such as houseless individuals or those struggling with addiction.
- Support awareness campaigns that combat stigma and remind the world that every missing person deserves to be found, no matter what their circumstances.

Keep Their Names Alive

Most importantly—don't forget the missing.

Share their stories, say their names, keep them alive in your hearts.

Michael was more than a case number. He was a brother, a friend, a man who loved Nascar and the ocean, someone who gave even when he had nothing. Every missing person has a story, a family, a life worth remembering.

A Message to Readers: Cherish Every Moment

Life moves fast. Too fast. It's easy to get caught up in responsibilities, in routines, in the day-to-day obligations that seem endless. But time? Time is never endless. If there's one lesson Michael's life has taught me, it's this: love people while you have them. Say the words. Make a call. Take the trip. Sit in silence together when words aren't needed.

We assume there will be more time. More chances. But sometimes, life doesn't give us the extra days we thought we had. And the only thing that remains is memory—the sound of their laughter, the way their voice filled a quiet room, the small gestures that once seemed ordinary but, in hindsight, were the most beautiful details of all.

Michael gave. Always. Without hesitation. He found joy in simple things, a fishing rod in his hands, music in his ears, the roar of a Nascar crowd, the way the ocean could take every worry and pull it into the tide. He loved fully, openly, without fear. That's what I want to pass on to you—to live that way, to love that way. Because in the end, the moments we make with those we cherish are the ones that stay.

So please, call your loved ones today. Tell them you love them—not tomorrow, not someday—today.

Because sometimes, today is all we get.

In Loving Memory

Michael David Long
(Forever 48)
Born June 9, 1971
At Saint John's Hospital, Santa Monica, California
Last call July 23rd, 2019

Loved. Missed. Gone to Soon. Never forgotten.

He is now my guardian Angel
I love you Lil Brother till we meet again

Author's Note

Writing this book broke my heart but gave it purpose. This is a way to memorialize Michael since his remains have never been found and not sure they ever will, especially if he was thrown in the ocean, or buried someplace on Maui hidden away.

Maui is very brushy. I know some people were close to Michael who knew what happened to him, and they betrayed him. People who were close to him made him disappear. They dimmed his light. He defiantly did not go missing on his own accord I know in my heart who is behind it and God certainly knows and they will have to answer to the higher source one day

Michael was more than my brother, he was kind, funny, selfless, and a soul full of life. His disappearance in July 2019 shattered our family, and the silence of his unsolved murder weighs heavily.

As of June 9th, 2025, his case remains open, stalled on its fourth or fifth detective, but no closure, and still listed as a missing person's case.

Michael mattered, and so do all missing people lost to criminal acts.

This memoir honors Michael and lifts those missing and the families waiting in limbo.

I've learned so much through this journey—not just about Michael, but about myself, about resilience, about the power of love and memory. I've connected with other families, shared tears and laughter, and found a community I never knew I needed. I've also seen the flaws in our systems, the ways we fail the most vulnerable, and I'm committed to advocating for change.

The act of going missing is not classified as a crime, which highlights the need to revise existing laws. This lack of classification is why such cases are often not thoroughly investigated. Law enforcement agencies typically focus their investigations on recognized criminal activities.

To support missing persons cases, consider these resources:
National Missing and Unidentified Persons System (NamUs): A database for missing persons cases.
Website: https://www.namus.nij.ojp.gov
The Doe Network: A volunteer organization for missing people and unidentified remains.
Website: https://www.doenetwork.org
The Charley Project: A database of missing persons cases in the U.S.
Website: https://charleyproject.org
Missing on Maui - Michael David Long: A Facebook page for updates on Michael Long's case.

Made in the USA
Columbia, SC
02 July 2025